MW01109217

Earth Friends

at
School

Francine Galko

Heinemann Library
Chicago, Illinois

© 2004 Heinemann Library
a division of Reed Elsevier Inc.
Chicago, Illinois

Customer Service   888–454–2279

Visit our website at www.heinemannlibrary.com

Designed by Anna Matras/Heinemann Library
Illustration by Carrie Gowran
Printed and bound in Hong Kong and China
by South China Printing Company Limited

08 07 06 05 04
10 9 8 7 6 5 4 3 2 1

**Library of Congress
Cataloging-in-Publication Data**
A copy of the cataloging-in-publication data for
this title is on file with the Library of Congress.
  Earth friends at school / Francine Galko.
  ISBN 1-4034-4897-3 (library binding-hardcover) --
  1-4034-4902-3 (pbk.)

Acknowledgments
The author and publisher are grateful to the
following for permission to reproduce copyright
material: p. 4 Richard Hamilton Smith/Corbis;
pp. 5, 6, 10, 11, 12, 13, 14, 15, 16, 17, 18, 19, 20,
21, 22, 23, 24, 25. 30 Warling Studios/Heinemann
Library; pp. 8, 29 Richard Hutchings/Photo Edit; p. 9
Owen Franken/Corbis; p. 26 Chad Weckler/Corbis;
p. 27 Joe McDonald/Corbis; p. 28 David Young-
Wolff/Photo Edit

Photo research by Janet Lankford Moran

Cover photograph by Warling Studios/Heinemann
Library

Every effort has been made to contact copyright
holders of any material reproduced in this book.
Any omissions will be rectified in subsequent
printings if notice is given to the publisher.

Some words are
shown in bold,
like this. You can
find out what they
mean by looking
in the glossary.

To learn about the picture on
the front cover, turn to page 11.

Contents

What Is an Earth Friend?

Earth friends use **natural resources** carefully. Natural resources are important **materials** found in nature. Air, water, land, and trees are natural resources.

This girl is sorting used paper
so that it can be used again.

Earth friends use only what they need.
They do not waste natural resources.
Earth friends also help keep Earth clean.

Earth's Resources

Earth has many **natural resources.** We use them every day. For example, trees are used to make paper, pencils, and schoolbooks. Some resources can be **replaced.** You can plant a new tree if one is cut down.

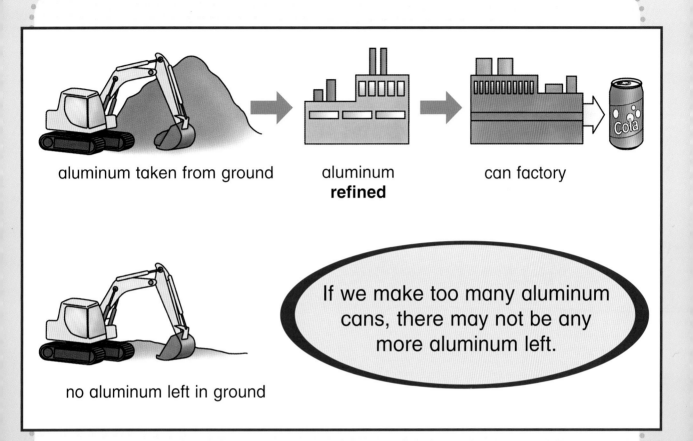

aluminum taken from ground

aluminum **refined**

can factory

no aluminum left in ground

If we make too many aluminum cans, there may not be any more aluminum left.

Other natural resources cannot be replaced. If we use them up, they are gone forever. Drink cans are made of **aluminum. Metals** such as aluminum can be used up if we do not use them wisely.

Getting to and from School

If you live near your school, try not to use the car. Cars use **gasoline,** which **pollutes** the air. Ask your parents if you can walk or ride your bike to school.

Some people live far from school. And sometimes the weather is bad. Try to share a ride with someone else. You can ride with a neighbor or ride the school bus.

In the Classroom

Talk with your classmates about ways to be Earth friends. You can take turns switching off the lights when everyone leaves the room.

Share your ideas with other people at school. Make a poster with your ideas. Ask for your teacher's help.

In the Cafeteria

Many lunch **containers** are **recyclable.**
Glass bottles, **plastic** bottles, and **aluminum**
cans can be recycled. Set up bins in the
school cafeteria for these **materials.**

Pack your lunch in containers that can be used again or recycled. This **reduces** the garbage that goes to **landfills.**

In the Library

Library books are used again and again.

In the library, students share books, magazines, and newspapers. By sharing **materials,** you **conserve** paper and trees.

used magazines

Some school libraries will take your used magazines and books. Then other people can use them. This keeps the magazines and books out of **landfills.**

On the Playground

Help keep your school playground clean. Put papers and other litter in a trash can. If there is no trash can nearby, put your trash in your pocket. Throw it away later.

This playground slide is made from recycled milk and water bottles.

Ask your school to buy recycled **materials** for the playground. Recycled tires can be used to make a soft pad for the playground. This kind of pad lasts for a long time.

Recycling at School

Some schools already **recycle.** Help your school recycle cans, bottles, and paper. Other schools do not recycle. You can help start a recycling **program.**

recycled paper

Talk to your teachers about using **recycled materials** in the classroom. Everyone can use recycled paper at school.

Using Less Paper

Ask your teacher if you can write on both sides of the paper. This will **reduce** the amount of paper you use. Less paper will go to the **landfill**.

This boy is using both sides of the paper.

Talk to your teachers about using less
paper. Teachers can use both sides of
a handout, too.

Arts and Crafts at School

Art class is fun. But some paints, markers, and glues use strong **chemicals.** These chemicals are not good for Earth or for you. Use **nontoxic** art **materials.**

You do not need special materials to make art. Ask your art teacher to use everyday things. These materials can be made into **eco-art.** Eco-art **reduces** trash, too.

To see how you can make a mobile from old CDs, turn to page 30.

Reusing School Supplies

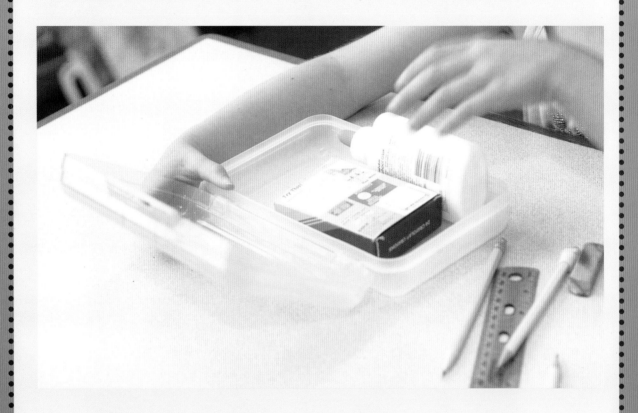

Reuse crayons, rulers, and other school supplies. You can use many school supplies from year to year. You do not need new ones every year.

Talk to your teachers about reusing things. Paper clips, thumbtacks, and rubber bands can be **collected** and used again.

Gardening for Wildlife

Some schools have butterfly gardens. These gardens give homes to butterflies and birds. Ask teachers and students to plant a butterfly garden at your school.

Some butterflies like to feed on certain kinds of plants.

bird feeder

These gardens have plants that butterflies like. Add bird feeders to your garden, too. Use a **field guide** to learn about the birds and butterflies in the garden.

Gardening for Food

You can grow fruits and vegetables in a school garden. Work together with teachers and students. Plant and take care of the garden.

Garden plants grow better with **compost.**
You can use food scraps from the cafeteria or
grass clippings from the lawn. Put them in a
compost pile. Then add them to your garden.

Activity: Make a Mobile

1. Ask your teacher and classmates to help find some CDs that no one wants.

2. Paint the shiny side of the CD with nontoxic paint.

3. Let the paint dry.

4. Scratch designs onto them.

5. Use string and old coat hangers to hang the CDs up, creating a mobile.

Glossary

aluminum kind of light metal

chemical material made from two or more other materials

collect gather or bring together

compost recycled yard waste and food scraps

conserve use less of a natural resource

container box or bottle used to hold something

eco-art art made from recycled material

field guide book that helps you find out the name of a living thing and learn more about it

gasoline liquid fuel used to power cars and other machines

landfill place where garbage is buried

material what a thing is made of

metal hard material found deep in the ground

natural resource important material found in nature

nontoxic free of harmful materials

plastic material made from coal or oil, water, and a kind of rock

pollute put harmful materials into the air, water, or ground

program plan for doing something

recycle collect materials so they can be used again

reduce use or make less

refine make something ready for use

replace put something new in the place of an old thing

reuse use again

More Books to Read

Jacobs, Francine. *Follow That Trash: All about Recycling.* New York: Penguin Putnam, 1996.

Oxlade, Chris. *Metal.* Chicago: Heinemann Library, 2001.

Index